I0521754

Rock The Mic(ronesia):

The
New Generation
of
Native Tongues

edited by
Sinangån-ta Outreach

Copyright© 2010 Sinangan-ta Outreach

All rights reserved.

This publication may not be reproduced, stored in a retrieval system, or transmitted in any form or by any means, electronic, mechanical, photocopying, recording, or otherwise, without prior written permission of the publisher, except by a reviewer who may quote brief passages in a review to be printed in a periodical.

Published by:

blue ocean press, an Imprint of Aoishima Research Institute (ARI)
#807-36 Lions Plaza Ebisu
3-25-3 Higashi, Shibuya-ku
Tokyo, Japan 150-0011

URL: http://www.aoishima-research.com

ISBN: 978-4-902837-40-7

Cover Design by Kie Susuico

This book is funded in part by grant from the Guam Humanities Council and the National Endowment for the Humanities. Any views, findings, conclusions, or recommendations expressed in this project do not necessarily represent those of the National Endowment for the Humanities and the Guam Humanities Council.

KONSEHILON
TINAOTAO
GUAM

GUAM
HUMANITIES
COUNCIL

Table of Contents

Introduction by Dr. Anne Perez Hattori 1

Foreword by Dr. Evelyn Flores 4

Chels 7

Christian Camacho 10

Mariah R. Flores 20

Isha Gabriel 25

Chanice Guevara 30

Sirena Mafnas 33

Asa Gonzalez-Peterson 39

Shane Salas 43

Peter Santos 50

John Norman "Metaforce" Sarmiento 55

Jessie Rae "J RAE" Tedtaotao 67

Verna Zafra 88

Organizers' Biographies 95

Acknowledgements 96

Photos 97-101

Hurao's Children

Despite what PDN, K57, and the Chamber of Commerce say,

Guam is not a rock.

Guam is not a military base.

Guam is not a dump.

Thousands of years before the United States became a nation, Chamorro civilization reigned over these islands that we now call the Marianas. Our long and deep history includes millions of experiences and memories, collected over 4,000 years of civilization, that describe our suffering and joy, hope and despair, laughter and sorrow. Our stories recount our experiences through typhoons and droughts, wars and epidemics, conflicts and rivalries. In our stories, we reminisce about fiestas and rosaries, barbecues at the beach, and the brilliant beauty of sunsets and flame trees. Our stories describe families functional and dysfunctional, unified and disunified, and, perhaps above all, resilient and adaptable.

While our rich and eventful past matches anyone's in this world, for hundreds of years our stories have been suppressed. Not only did colonizers steal our governments, but they also committed a cultural robbery, rejecting our stories in favor of their own. These colonial stories differ from ours in many important ways – for one, they get to be the heroes, leaving us on the villainous end of the stick. In their accounts, we wind up looking inferior, described as thieves and/or savages and/or childlike and/or corrupt and/or insert-you-own-negative-description.

Another important way in which colonial story-telling differs dramatically from ours is the treatment of written and oral sources. Like all other Islanders in Oceania, and most of the world, for that matter, the Chamorro people tell our stories and keep our history in oral formats. Pacific Islanders use chants, songs, and proverbs to remember important information. For example, chants that tell the directions to navigate from one Micronesian island to another have been maintained with accuracy for hundreds, possibly thousands, of years. Some islanders use tattoos to tell their personal and clan histories, and we all use story-telling and speech-making. Slam Poetry fuses together many of these oral traditions, representing a form of oratory that fits neatly within the body of Pacific oral tradition. The constellation of oral formats has enabled us to entertain and educate ourselves with lively descriptions of our experiences, and, in the process, pass on essential knowledge to succeeding generations. Through our oral traditions, we express who we are and what is important to us as individuals, as families, as clans, and as a people.

But our colonizers ridiculed these oral traditions, instead viewing their written documents as more accurate and legitimate. Rather than honoring Puntan and Fu'una as Gods who created the world, we were taught to reject them as superstitious, primitive myths and instead honor a single christian god. Instead of honoring Mata'pang, Agualin, and the maga'håga as leaders of our island, we learned about Magellan, San Vitores, Washington, and Kennedy. Whether our oral accounts described cultural, social, political, or economic matters, they were uniformly tossed aside as unreliable, unsophisticated, and primitive. Instead, written accounts, many of dubious merit, became elevated as "primary sources" in the understanding of all things Chamorro.

Since Chamorro contact with the West in the 17th century, individuals such as maga'lahe Hurao understood the destructive consequences of respecting written over oral sources. In his brilliant 1671 battle speech, he stated, "They treat our history as fable and fiction. Haven't we the same right concerning that which they teach us as incontestable truths?" Hurao rejected outright the supremacy of Western history and knowledge, asserting the Chamorro right to tell our stories in our ways. In this oratorical piece, Hurao called on his supporters, "Let us not lose courage .... We are stronger than we think!"

More than 300 years and three colonizers later, we have not lost or forgotten our way. The outstanding success of the Sinangån-ta

Outreach provides clear, 21st century proof that oral traditions live on, as strongly and passionately as if Hurao himself were in our modern midst.

Read these poems, and read them out loud, as they were born to be spoken. Read these poems, and hear today's issues and concerns. Read these poems, and connect to a 4,000 year old tradition of oratory that colonial land-grabbing and body-snatching cannot extinguish.

Sinangån-ta
Tell your stories, and they become ours.

Tell your stories, and they inspire us to be courageous and bold.

Tell your stories, and they speak for our time and place in this world.

Tell your stories, and we remember that we are Hurao's children, that

   Guam is not a rock,

   Guam is not a military base,

   Guam is not a dump.

   Guam is our home and homeland, the only one we've got.

Biba i Sinangån-ta Outreach, especiatmente si Melvin, si Kie, yan si Fanai.

Anne Perez Hattori,

University of Guam

Professor, History

Foreward

The idea of the Sinangån-ta Youth Outreach Program began with three young writers who understood that in the transition from oral to written literacy, many of our island's youth had lost their bearings. These young people were adrift with no land in sight. They did not trust the elitist world of "standard" English but had no other platform from which to speak. And yet they were desperate to speak, to shout out their anger, their confusion at a world that often betrayed them but also their joy at unexpected friendships, love, and beauty. What space was there for them? And how would the act of speaking save their lives? The answer for the three writers grew through the years as each in his or her own way experienced Spoken Word events that convinced them that here was the outlet they sought for Guam youth. Summoning the support of friends, acquaintances and relatives who also felt this huge need, they planned, had meetings, fund-raised, and persisted through overwhelming disappointments to turn their vision into reality.

As I sat and listened to J Rae Tedtaotao, the winner of Sinangån-ta 's 2009 Last Word Poetry Slam, I understood why poetry slamming has been called a contact sport. Not only is there a powerful "slamming " together of emotion very much like two bodies colliding, but there is also a powerful "slam" of understanding as audience and poet together ride a monster wave of merciless confusion onto a long, white beach of meaning and understanding.

J Rae won the The Last Word Slam not just for her spectacular performance but for the truth of her words: There are other ways to deal with rage than through violence, drugs, and mayhem—through writing, she saved her life. "I picked up my pen," she testifies, "and found my peace through writing!" The words rang through my mind for several days along with the desperation from which they came.

From this perspective, Melvin, Kie, and Fanai, the organizers of

Sinangån-ta and its after-school program have also "made contact"—with students in school who had been alienated from the written page, with youth angry at society's abysmal failures and its grotesque cover-ups, with parents and friends, uncles, and aunts, nieces, and nephews who by experiencing the power of slam began to renew their own commitments to speak up.

But most of all, these three impassioned visionaries made contact with a part of our island culture that is gravely threatened by high-speed living—our oral traditions. When I saw young writers showing up at a Sinajana Community Center when they could have been out with friends, laptops, and texting on cellphone, when I heard not only Jrae but John Sarmiento, Isha, Shane, Sirena, and all the others, I realized Sinangån-ta had slam-dunked its way into an idea for preserving our culture. It wasn't Kantan Chamorrita by any stretch of the imagination, but it was its equivalent with its good-natured, edgy, competitive performance, youthfulness, cheering audience, and words----flying, singing, entangling, ricocheting words that pulled no punches but only tried as honestly as possible to speak the truth of experience, however slippery that might be.

The pages that follow are the written evidence of over two years' worth of effort on the part of Sinangån-ta's organizers. But for the youth poets whose works are published here, it's much more than that. It's a door they've broken open. And they're walking in. Slam!

by Dr. Evelyn Flores

Associate Professor, Pacific Island Literature

University of Guam

Heller, I'm Chelsea Santos.
16.Tamuning.JFK

"I know it'll be all right in the end as long as I can focus my fears and channel my life through my pen"

-- CunninLynguists

I walked into school with puffy eyes from only 3 hours of sleep thinking that **you** were gonna be there.
The night before was bull and i most definitely needed you to comfort me.
Instead, you skipped first block and found comfort in a
THC-filled 20-dollar joint.
I was walking towards you and i knew automatically..
You were **Blowwnnn.**
I looked into your dark red eyes and at that moment i wanted to slam your head up against the concrete wall.
I mean, 'Are you serious?'
Do you remember saying to me that weed was a bad habit?
We even made an agreement to stop. It isn't a necessity in my life.
But obviously it's a different story for you.
Smiling, Bouncing up and down like a little first grader.
It was tempting. I really wanted to kick your ass.
And i don't mean just punch you.
I wanted to kick your balls, do a quadruple karate chop, and make
sure your head was so swollen it looked like a damn basketball.
Oddly, I kept my cool.
After a while I felt bad for you.
I wanted to embrace you
because sometimes you really don't know what the hell you're doing.
Even if you don't see it.. So many people have faith in you.
You're throwing your opportunities out the window!
I mean look at you. Your heart is WAY bigger than your face.
You're amazing and brilliant.
You happened to help me realize that life is more precious than it seems.
That words are stronger than actions.
And Love...brings out the **real** person inside of you.
When the day comes and you see in yourself
that you have this extraordinary amount of potential
no one that you want will be there.. Except ME.

I will never give up on you.
I will never leave you when you're at your lowest point in life.
I will never turn my back on you.
I will **forever** open my heart to yours..

Because Love is like a gamble.

And **I'll bet it all on you**.

Christian Jon Leo Dydasco Camacho

17
Santa Rita
Southern High School

Influences:
Past and present English teachers, Def Poetry Jam, Brave New Voices, friends, and family.

Why I write:
I never started writing seriously until about two years ago. Most of my writing was personal and to me corny, and unworthy of any type of audience. It wasn't until one of my most influential teachers introduced me to "Spoken Word Poetry" and "Def Poetry Jam", that I learned that my writing didn't have to matter to anyone else, but me. I have since learned to express myself through my writing and it has become a creative outlet for me, and has given me the strength and courage to do things and say things I have never be able to say out loud before in my life. I write because it has become a passion, it has become almost second nature to me and without it I would probably go crazy!

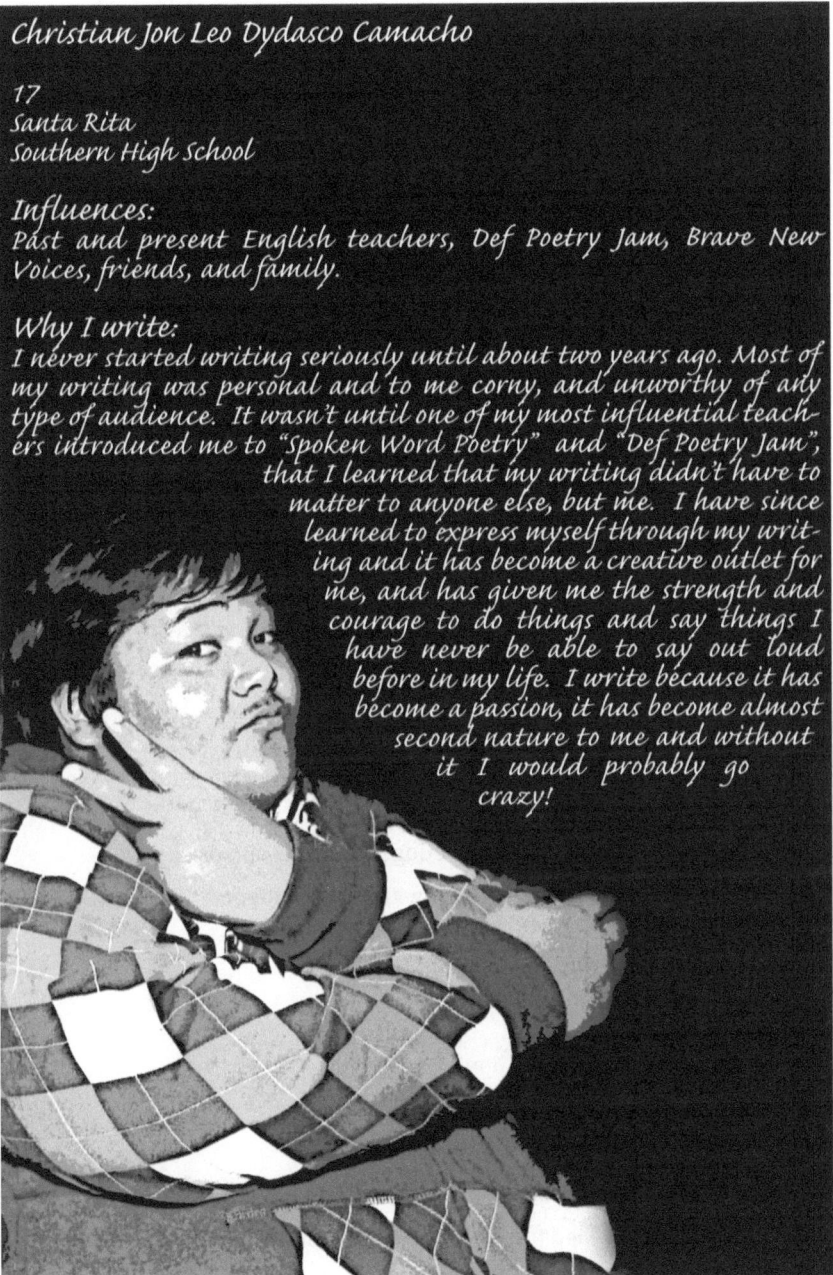

Amber

It isn't her fault

no one ever told her to go outside

to play with the other kids because now she is unable to.

'Cause self-consciousness,

short breaths,

and up**hill** battles

are now playing their part

in stopping her from living her life.

*

See exercise,

runnnnnnnnnnnning

and day long crash diets

cause her to binge

over

and

over

again

less eating, not eating, diet foods and drinks

aren't working at least not for her

*

Slim fast,

slim quick

don't do Shhhhhh…it

for people who aren't well...

slim

'cause diet pills and death-trap machinery won't change **her size**~~size~~.

and trust me when I say she has tried.

*

working out never "worked out" for her
She convinced herself it wasn't her fault

See 'cause the king,

the queen,

the colonel,

the clown

and that damn

Wendy girl

were her problem

like it was peer pressure or something

*

like some poor girl being forced to

smoke a burger,

sniff that chicken wing,

and eat 'til her jaw fell off.

tempting her with games she couldn't win,

toys that came free with the meal,

and tricking her with that

juicy

never

frozen

beef

that never looked anything like in the commercial.

*

Not knowing that the double quarter pounder with the large fries and a shake
Came with a   price and trust me when I say heavy.

Heavy

*

But it's been a long time and all she sees is
people around her getting smaller and smaller.

Following those subliminal messages in

TV,

movies,

and magazines seeping their

>skinny<

ways in to the mind of this young girl who sees every guy to the left and right
of her is wanting

10,

no 15,

wait no 20 pounds

less than what she had.

Almost desperately looking for love but boys are too shallow minded to think
twice about her.

So at 135 pounds at 5'3 she developed a complex that she was too fat.

*

And then with a blade and a bad day she was gone.

playing it off like no one wanted her

like the world would be better off without her

not knowing it would send her family in to a downward spiral of long term
pain.

Not knowing how much pain she had caused

while they watched

their daughter,

their sister,

their niece,

MY FRIEND

being

buried.

*

She was a friend of mine long gone from Guam,

desperately crying to come home.

She befriended me when no one else did.

She was there for the good times and the bad times,

even those in between times.

I cried on the phone asking her mother

why?

*

She said all she left was a note and it said:

"Mom it's time for me to leave. I'm sorry I couldn't be the **beautiful** daughter
you always wanted."

Not knowing that we loved

her beautiful smile,

her loving attitude

and

her comedic look on life.

*

I wondered to myself "was there something I could have done?"

*

Could I have been there for her more?

*

Could I have sent more letters than I did?

*

Could I have called more?

*

Would it have made a difference?

*

Would my contact have changed her choice of relief?

*

I only wish I had talked to her more.

Unspoken Word 2

He was a loner who sat by himself at school

Flew solo through

      classes,
           lunch,

         and life...

       *

The one with looks of desperation making him
Unapproachable and in every sense of the word, a *freak*

*

Quietly screaming for someone to see him
And at home it was no different
He played music to drown out the yelling
A broken-**ho me** kid scared of what will happen next

*

His mother always fighting with his step dad
He watched as they buried

his brother

A drive by shooting that drained him of his life
and took with him the life of his family

*

And drugs from that day on infecting his mother
One day he did not come home
Packed his bag and jumped the late train to anywhere that wasn't called home
Running away from the loneliness he felt
From the screaming mouths, the clenched fists, and his past life

that he shall never speak of again

*

CHRISTIAN CAMACHO

She was the daddy's girl who wore long sleeves to hide

the bruises,

cuts,

and cigarette burns

on her arms

*

See she came from a family that was taught by a

Drunken daddy that discipline came with a cost

Bruises

and

scars,

the price,

paid for

nothing

*

This was the girl you saw sitting with a laughing group of friends

But was the only one *silent* because broken ribs made it too hard to join in on
the fun

The only one with

a black hoodie

_____

over her head

praying that her friends wouldn't question

Her choice of style

*

That night she came home to see

Daddy sitting drenched in **blood**

and intoxicated by love but not the love for his daughter

instead intoxicated by the love of

SIXTEEN

12

bottles

of

beer

and

3

bottles

vodka

laying on the living room floor waiting for more love to show up

*

He was drunk and she was scared

Her mother was nowhere to be seen

She saw the blood and ran

Locked herself in her room screaming for help

But no one came

Only the police to relieve her of her problems

Answering complaints made by neighbors

So now everyone knows what really happened

Everyone knows who did it

*

Her name plastered all over

TV's

and

newspapers

These were the kids who didn't feel like talking

The ones you

Couldn't

Wouldn't

And didn't

say anything to

Who

didn't

think

that

there

was

a good enough solution

*

Now they are nowhere to be found

He's long gone, changed his name and is now playing that game

turning SKCIRTTRICKS as if it was a professional trade

And she is far away from home but living in the same house

*

Without her parents for the first time and she is scared to be

*

ALONE

*

These were the kids that at one point or another in their lives were happy

but the problems of life

and the poisons of Family

had taken over everything

they knew and they had nowhere to turn

And now the only thing

left in the_____empty spaces

they used_____to call their

lives Are

unspoken words

lingering in vain as the world goes on as if nothing happened

*

But with you

CHRISTIAN CAMACHO

I see it everyday you walk in before me and you are upset,
The pain welling up from inside
Screaming for someone to hear you
Hoping that someone will tell you everything is going to be all right
I know the reasons why, but all I can do is offer you an ear
So please
*

speak

Mariah R. Flores

14 yrs old
Malesso'
Southern High School, IMS Graduate

Influences:
The people who influence my life are my mom, my grandfather, my brothers, my teachers, and my friends.

Why I write:
I write because it helps me relieve stress, and it helps me express how I feel.

I have fallen for you for the last time
No more getting hurt
No more saying *"I LOVE YOU"*
because you have hurt me for the last time
I can't stand up straight thinking that you will change
I can't wait there wishing you would give me another chance
because you have hurt me too many times
I always had to take your side over everyone else's
I just had to say "yes" once more

The first time I was **falling**

The second time I was there

The third time I was **in love**

But I guess that you were too blind to see that I was **real** and **true**
You really wouldn't know how it feels to have your heart broken in two
And I guess that you really don't have enough feelings to cry
You weren't the one crying to your friends telling them everything,

I was

I just have to wonder what got me all those times

was it your good looks, your charm?

or was it just your sweet talk?

I wonder why you asked three times and then hurt me?

I also have to ask myself
why was I so drawn to you?
why couldn't I just say "no, no, no, no?"

I think now I know why I said yes,
because I thought that you had changed your ways and
saw that I was real
But I guess all that pain that you put me through has shown
me
that I don't really need someone like you in my life
after all
My friends were right about you, that you are nothing but
a good looking player
I am so happy that I have friends that will have my back
no matter what I do
even if they don't approve
I would say that I always cared about you,

but then I would be un**real** and un**true** if I did,

so **I won't.**

I didn't want to be the one who feels the way one should when
they like that person
Yes, I like you
and no, I don't want to fall and have no one there to catch me
You drive me wild with every kiss and I feel as if I never want to
let go

I want
you to be there for me at all times to support me

I don't want
your ex-girlfriend to put me down thinking that I am not good
enough for you

Looking at all those pictures of **you** and her make **me** feel like I
could do those things too,
but I'm not her
and

I don't want to be like her

I don't want to be something I'm not

I don't want to be a "*wanna be*"

because all I want to be

is me

making you happy
I want you to make me happy
I don't want her to get in the way of me being with you because

I'm in **love** with yo**u**

I don't want to dream every night of something wrong
All I want to dream of is us happy together

that's all I want

I don't want to be the type of person I was before with all the
others
because you are different from them
You have something they don't

You have **me**

and that's all you need

I'm not a perfect person, but I'll do my best to love you
Just one look is not enough to last me the days I spend without
you
I start to miss you once my eyes leave you

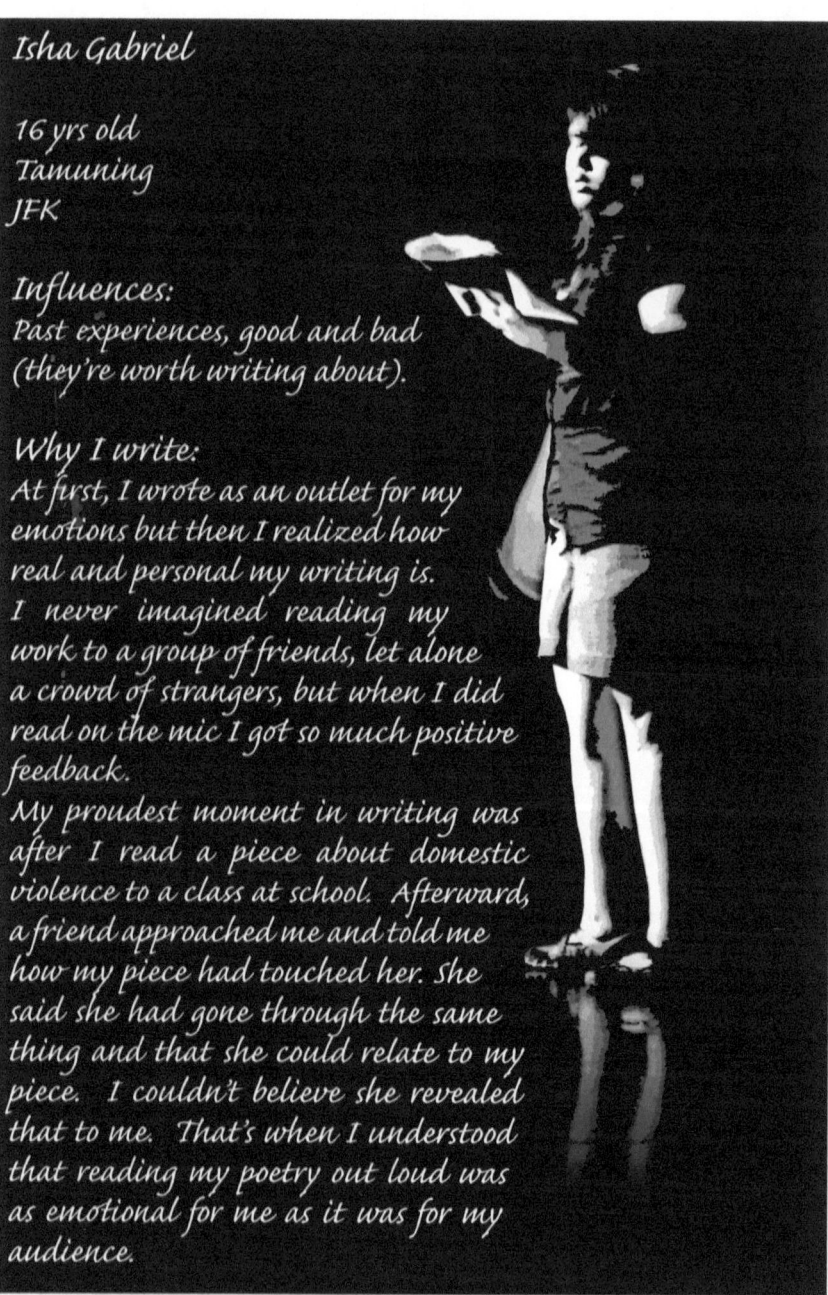

Isha Gabriel

16 yrs old
Tamuning
JFK

Influences:
Past experiences, good and bad
(they're worth writing about).

Why I write:
At first, I wrote as an outlet for my
emotions but then I realized how
real and personal my writing is.
I never imagined reading my
work to a group of friends, let alone
a crowd of strangers, but when I did
read on the mic I got so much positive
feedback.
My proudest moment in writing was
after I read a piece about domestic
violence to a class at school. Afterward,
a friend approached me and told me
how my piece had touched her. She
said she had gone through the same
thing and that she could relate to my
piece. I couldn't believe she revealed
that to me. That's when I understood
that reading my poetry out loud was
as emotional for me as it was for my
audience.

Her Last Night

Your rage got the better of you tonight.

You call yourself a man?

Well, I have never heard of a man that can meet his **fists** with a woman's **face**.

I've never heard of a man who could use his **strength** against the **woman** who loves him.

I've never heard of a man who could feel **no regret** but still offer an **empty apology**.

But she'll accept it.

Even though she knows that your sorries are as hollow as your heart.

You were once her lover.

The only time you'd raise your fist would be to defend her.

But soon enough, you turned on her.

She watched the man she wanted to share her life with turn into a monster

as quickly as that liquor poured down his throat.

And as soon as that monster surfaced,

it wasn't long before she was on the floor once again feeling the sting of his strike.

Oh, but how he loves the high he gets from being unstoppable.

No, she can't stop you.

All she can do is lay there and pray to God that she makes it out of this one.

And she does.

But how much of that woman died at your hand that night?

She uses her surviving strength to walk into the bathroom and clean herself up.

She would not dare peer into the mirror for fear of what she'd see.

Not bruises or blood, but the eyes of a woman no longer recognizable

the eyes of a woman whose joy and spirit were beaten out of her

The only trace of humanity left is that cross she wears around her neck.

This is a familiar sight to her.

But this time is different.

This time, instead of feeling pain, she is consumed with anger.

"*Is this what he's made of me?!*"

"*Is this what I've let myself become?!*"

Her clenched fist shatters the mirror.

This feels like a vivid dream as she storms out the room.

She approaches her husband and before he can scream an obscenity,

he's on the floor begging at her hand

not begging for his life but begging for her to stay.

And before he can blurt out another "baby please,"

she's out the door

and this nightmare is about to become a memory.

But not just any memory.

She'll carry every slap, every tear, every sleepless night with her.

But they will not consume her.

They will only make her stronger.

Isha Gabriel

Photo-Finish

A stack of binded pages in front of me.

My hand's shaking,

anticipating.

Like a car at the starting line.

All this potential energy

held in this pen

ready to **explode**

on these soon-to-be inked pages.

My heart's racing, adrenaline rushing.

Better than drugs, sex, and any combination of the two.

The start flag waves in my mind.

The skanky flag girl moves out of the way

because she knows what's about to go down.

My hand's about to go into auto-pilot.

Everything on my mind is about to be illustrated on these milky white sheets.

The only things keeping me contained

are these <u>thin blue lines</u> and red-ish, pink-ish |margins.|

My mind dishes out these words and my hand tries to keep up.
I savor every moment.
Every word and punctuation.
I have no time for indentations.
My hand is falling behind.
I forget about "penmanship";

and all those grammar lessons from 1st period English.
I have no time.
No time for that eraser
if I make a mistake
I jump the speed bump and keep going.
I see the finish line and all of a sudden,
a flat tire.

My mind goes crazy as the pit crew scrambles for the spare.

The whole time I'm in the driver's seat trying not to scream.

I wana throw the pen against the wall and yell "**what's your problem!?**"

but I have to finish this race against my memory.
I pull from the back of my mind, a line that makes this piece
original, unfounded, and precious to me.
Then I thank God when I'm finished.

It was a photo-finish and I made that writer's block kiss my bumper!

I made that finish line suck my exhaust.

I'm staring down at my little labor of love

thinking to myself, "don't change a thing."

This is perfection personified.

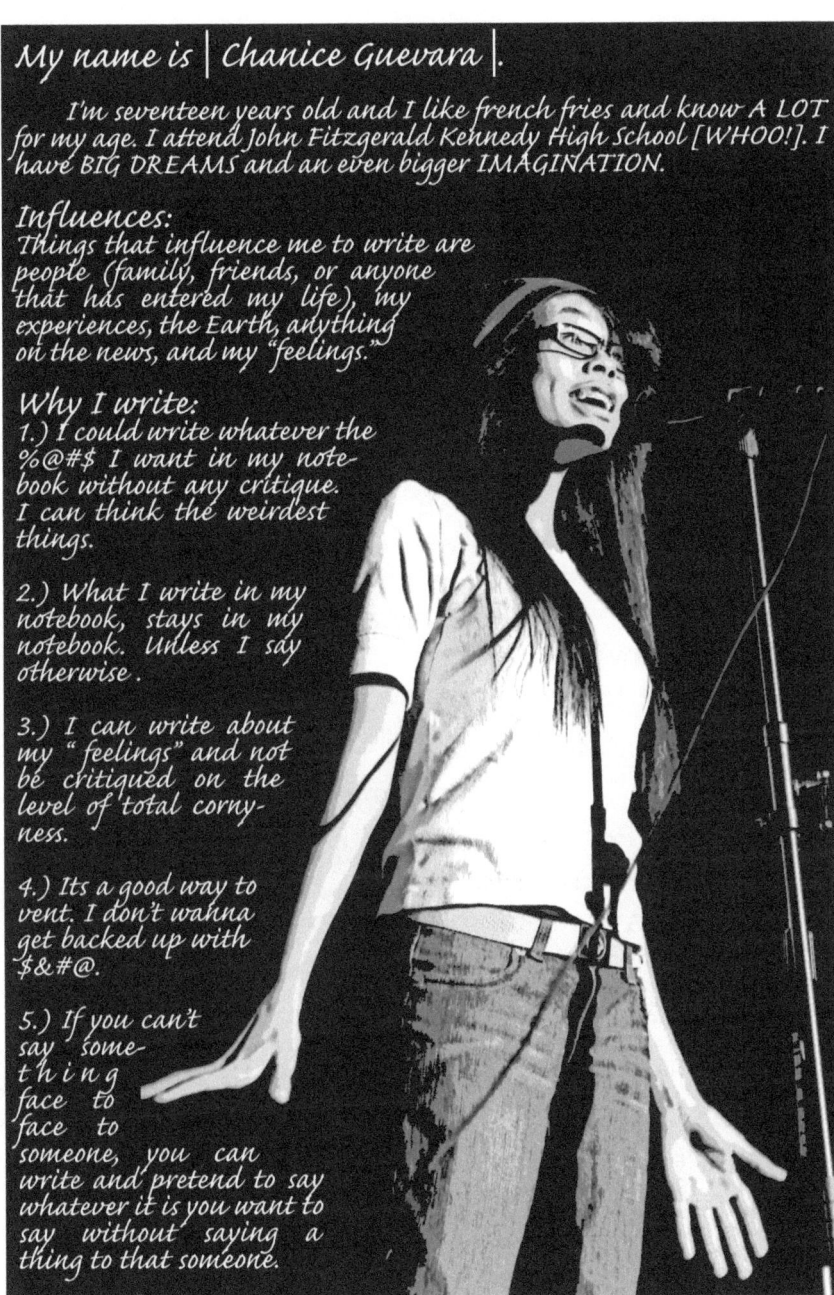

My name is | Chanice Guevara |.

I'm seventeen years old and I like french fries and know A LOT for my age. I attend John Fitzgerald Kennedy High School [WHOO!]. I have BIG DREAMS and an even bigger IMAGINATION.

Influences:
Things that influence me to write are people (family, friends, or anyone that has entered my life), my experiences, the Earth, anything on the news, and my "feelings."

Why I write:
1.) I could write whatever the %@#$ I want in my notebook without any critique. I can think the weirdest things.

2.) What I write in my notebook, stays in my notebook. Unless I say otherwise.

3.) I can write about my "feelings" and not be critiqued on the level of total cornyness.

4.) Its a good way to vent. I don't wahna get backed up with $&#@.

5.) If you can't say something face to face to someone, you can write and pretend to say whatever it is you want to say without saying a thing to that someone.

Dora

I am an explorer
And like other great explorers, I do not travel alone
I travel with my best friend
My best friend wears boots, which we call him
And did I mention that he is a monkey?
YES! He is an adorable naked monkey wearing Coke red boots
There is this sly fox
He is a swiper, which we call him
He always tries to swipe my stuff and when he does, he delays my adventures!
Then, I have to waste my time and try to find it

What an A-HOLE!

Excuse my Spanish!
Apparently, he doesn't like it when people say his name **tres** times in a row
"**TRES**" is the number 3 in Spanish
I, on the other hand, am a WIDE-eyed adorable girl
Children just love my WIDE eyes
They're my best feature!
I teach little children how to speak Spanish while taking them on one of my adventures!
I always have **tres** locations on my adventures.
Remember, "**TRES**" is the number 3 in Spanish
As an explorer, I always come prepared
I never leave home without my handy purple back pack

and trusty map
I wouldn't get through any of my adventures without them
Boots, Swiper, my Backpack AND my Map talk to me,
along with other adorable animals and inanimate objects.
I can't explain why though

Maybe it was in the days when I wasn't an explorer...

One day, I was walking to my **Abuela's** house.
"**Abuela**" is grandmother in Spanish
I took a shortcut through the woods,
and bumped into my friend Mary. Her last name is Jane.
She can free your mind and get you flying high, as HIGH
as the sky
Every morning, I say "hello" to Mary Jane, and become
the wonderful explorer I am today.

SO, Come On! Vamanos! Everybody Lets Go!

Today on my adventure, Swiper swiped my friend Mary,
and I couldn't seem to find her anywhere!
I looked over the mountain,
through the woods,
and now I'm going to check at my **Abuela's** house.

DING DONG

"**Abuela! Abuela!** Have you seen my friend, Mary?"

Abuela says, "No. but maybe this is a good thing."

"**Thanks Abuela....**"

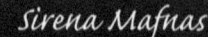

Sirena Mafnas

16
Talofofo

Influences:

I started writing poetry after I went to a poetry slam at school. I thought the poets who came to spit were amazing. They are the people that influenced me to write. My experiences and my need to be heard also influenced me to write. I found writing was the best way for me to be heard. Reading definitely played a big part in the reasons why I started writing, and last but not least, my best friend Kai, who also writes too. She helped and encouraged me so much.

Why I write:

I write to release all the things that are dying to leave my mind, and be read and understood by other people. I write to make my truth known. I write so that people who are experiencing the same things I am experiencing know that they're not alone.

My inspiration is my Sinangån-ta family, my mom and dad, my friends, and God.

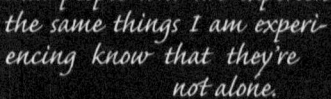

Glob of Tissue

My mom is 3 weeks pregnant and she wants to procure an
abortion.

Great.

Another death in my family.

The only difference is, this is expected.
You see, my father suddenly died when I was six
and that hurt more than sticks and stones could ever hurt.
My mother was kicked to the dirt because of his death
and since then her mind was bent and impaired.

It's been a week since I found out about the pregnancy.
She sat me down and told me her conspiracy.

She said, "I can't handle it. I can't mother it.

Besides, it's

just a fetus,

just a clump of cells,

just a glob of tissue."

Silence enfolded us like the zig-zags that wrap the tobacco
leaves she still smokes
even though she knows she's pregnant.
And I began to realize the message that she sent.

She called my baby brother or sister an "IT."

So was that all I was?

I shouted at her.
At her attempted murder.
She said it was legal in this society,

SO I SHOULD BE KILLED TOO MOM. She started to get pissed as I dissed her freedom, but mom, look at this **wonderful strong girl you've decided to bring into this world.** I can sing, dance, write, and draw. I have more friends than I do enemies. I have a 93% GPA, and people tell me, "Girl, you've got potential."

So think about the POTENTIAL YOU'RE HOLDING INSIDE OF YOU.
The next

GHANDI,

MARTIN LUTHER KING JR,

MOTHER TERESA,

Or

BARACK OBAMA

I just hate it that I have to remind you,
once upon a time 15 years ago

I...

was once that

GLOB OF TISSUE.

Downfall

When I look at you, you remind me how you made me seem stupid for the sake of your glorious splendor.

How your mind couldn't render your ability to be better.

But I waited for each so called "simple" aspect of YOU to be revealed to me because everything about you is…

beyond simplicity.

Beyond flowers simply blooming and leaves moving with the wind.

It was your smile when you said hello. The way your cheekbones lifted up the skin under your eyes,

Those beyond-simplicity-features were like thousands of supernovas happening all at once

Beautiful explosions coming into my life and creating in my head new solar systems of thoughts of what I would do for you.
No wonder why I stared past your egotistical pessimism.

Like stars burning through the atmosphere, you burned through my never-ending doubts and landed on my heart.

But at the same time, you treated me like the earth, throwing trash lies at my face,

and before I could ask "why?" you step on my mouth and walk away.

Like a driver under the influence

You drove recklessly on to my path to happiness and collided in to my dignity.

And as I lay on the road, broken, I watched you leave, and take it away from me.

I feel like you're kicking me,

Kicking me like a ball in a soccer game, only you've kicked me beyond the goal post because I wasn't that goal you wanted to score.

and yet,

you've somehow impregnated me with this love that I just can't let out of my system, like when Mozart couldn't let go of the rhythm in his head. And I hate it how for most men I've met, a lover is just a thing they look forward to in bed, as if a pillow and a TV set to channel 75 isn't already overrated.
For so long you've lived off a long drag of a

nicotine-filled marshmallow,

And the occasional erection from fantasies of your nightly routine.
I don't want to be your new friend on MySpace where the only conversation we'll ever have is, "Thanks for the add."
I DON'T WANT A PLATONIC FRIENDSHIP.
How can we pretend like this when I stare at you, and you stare at me for seconds that feel like hours?

Knowing we've confused short spaces of time with

Eternity.

I hate this inability to move my lips and talk to you. I'm tired of being helpless. I Want to project these verses and make you ferocious with complex compassion.

I want you.

I don't want that cigarette in your hand when you're mad, I want my hand there.

I don't want that **joint** on your lips when you want to feel ON TOP OF THE WORLD, I want my **lips** there.

You mean the $HEAVENS$ to me because this world tore us apart.

Now here is a special intention I hold in the silence of my heart:
I hope one day you will see the darkness in your reputation,

the consequence awaiting you.

When that day comes

I will run my hands over your eyes and lips,

Slide my arms underneath you,

And **hold you up**

In the moment of your

Downfall.

Asa Gonzalez-Peterson
16 yrs old
Asan

it's been said that the revolution won't be tell-a-vised(*lies*)

i guess we said screw it and modernized anyway

because Huxley's prophecies are just a stone's throw away for us to be
skipping across a pond of

books and loud noises
flowers and electric shocks

i mean it already seems to me that
dreams
have been reduced in size to fit megabytes
bits of ideas deleted to fit with what the norm of individuality has
become
real laughs and smiles formed into parenthesis and periods.   :)

it's not even like rebellion is canned anymore,

it's sent high-speed and broadbanned

so i think of revolution being born out of social unrest,
a test to urn what people felt was their turn to take,
but comfort has been industrialized and we are helped to

eat, and to

sleep, to

think, and to

have sex with

pills,

will
will

be kept rested and untested

i think of revoultions,

images crusading throughout my imagination,
like an imperialist nation,
the mixed bloody flesh
a gray stretched mesh

of "**CASUALTIES**" covering my brain
these "**NORMALITIES**" have been slain by a blade that is as
razor sharp
as we are vain

we have chosen a side that is disillusioned by ficticious differences,
that are worn as battle paint,
while battle cries
drip
from fearful eyes
into pools
as
unstoppable forces
absorbing
every
drop,
but it's gotten to the point that when these teardrops pop across its top,
that gloss won't ripple
accepting each and every one as a donation for its cause
all that, while biding time for some sort of conclusion,
those same moments could have been those fleeting experiences that get
away from us
more and more,
faster and faster they flee
like being bouyant in the ocean,
floating over the slow motions that cradle every curve,
while the wind tingles every nerve with
salt sprayed by the sea,

anxious

to see the different colors that will be strewn across the sky like a box of
colored yarn,
each strand tangled and turning twisting and yearning to beat each other

to the horizon.

it seems to me the sky is mocking us with its sunsets,
because no matter how you bet that race won't end,
it'll just stream on into a day
a new place
in a constant evolution of itself

so i think of revolutions and
i know that i won't see them
on t.v. or my computer screen

i'll see them coloring the streets
dancing and chanting to heart beats

Shane Salas

18
Hågat
Southern High School

Since the beginning of time violence has been upon us

From the time of the dinosaurs to the current war in Iraq and Afghanistan

Forever staring into your eyes and taking many different forms

From bombs dropping out of the sky killing thousands of innocent people

To starving kids around the world

Violence feels like the devil ripping your heart out when you have to watch your loved ones leave to fight a war, knowing their chances are slim

Leaving you sitting by the phone, waiting for that one call to let you know that they're ok.

Violence sounds like planes crashing into the twin towers and thousands of people yelling and crying for help.

It's military recruiters rolling into schools across the nation preaching that the military is the way to go.

They promise that you can go to school and make a lot of money and all you have to do is sign your life away.

Violence is CNN and Fox News focusing more on Anna Nicole Smith's death than children dying because they happen to live in a war zone.

It's marines in Okinawa raping women and destroying homes and the government thinks that bringing them to Guam will solve all our problems.

It's abusing our homeland for military training and storing

chemical weapons all-the-while keeping it a secret from the native people.

It's Uncle Sam pointing a crooked finger at you

Not saying, "I want you," but, "I NEED YOU."

"I need you to leave your family, your pregnant wife, and your unborn child to fight my war.
I need you to lace those boots, strap on that gun, and pull that trigger, killing a man you never even met.
A man who left his family for the same reasons you did."

And you WANT Uncle Sam.

Because he has the money that you need to feed your family.

Violence is Spain, Japan, and the U.S. of A. stepping foot on our island, changing our way of life, our beliefs, and cutting out our native tongues.

Its mothers having to work two jobs to put a hot plate on the dinner table and fathers having to work overtime to pay the bills on time

It's paying an arm and a leg to get a good education even when our people have already lost their arms and legs fighting for that same education.

Violence is putting a deadly AK47 in an 18 year-old's hands

And saying he's good enough to kill for his country but not good enough to be treated like a man.

It's putting children in foster homes 'cause mommy and daddy were so hungry for that next fix

That they forgot about their children starving at home, hoping that their love sticks.

Violence left Martin Luther King Jr. -- dead

Malcolm X -- dead

Ghandi -- dead

Che Guevara -- dead

Maga'lahi Matå'pang -- ma'puno

Jeromy Newby -- dead

And even Jesus Christ, the son of God, -- dead

Violence stinks of bodies rotting under piles of debris from a guided-missile that was misguided

It sounds like families crying and asking their god, "WHY?"

Violence sounds like George W. Bush continuing to read "My Pet Goat" even after he was informed that the nation was under attack.

He said that these colors don't run, and he was right

Because the only thing running was him.

Violence is presidents using the word freedom in their speeches when finding freedom is about as easy as finding Bin Laden.

And if you believe that we're dying because "Freedom ain't FREE"

Then open your eyes and realize that it   SHOULD BE.

But these days, the only thing that seems to be free is VIOLENCE.

SHANE SALAS

My Best Friend

I met my best friend in kindergarten
her name was Susie,
brown skin,
white dress,
and dimples on her cheeks when she smiled,
the cutest little girl you've ever seen.

We did everything together as we grew up.
Smiles were endless
everyday around 10 o'clock
we would meet up in the playground at the park.
For hours playing freeze tag,
goofing around on the monkey bars,
having a great time as always.

It was two days until her 10th birthday,
when I went over to her house and helped her plan her
birthday party.
She told me that she wanted this day to be the best day of her life,
a day she will never forget.
On the day of her party everything went great,
fun games and all her friends came over.
The day was everything she imagined it to be
the sun shined bright, as laughter flowed through the air.

The day after, I went to the park to meet up with Susie and she
wasn't there.
A week went by and I hadn't heard from her once,
so I decided to go over to her house.
I knocked on the door and Susie's mom answered

"Is Susie here?"

I saw her face as I had never seen it before

the bottom of her eyes got puffy
and tears were started dripping down her face.

"She moved in with her grandparents,"
the look on her face told me that something was wrong
I knew Susie wouldn't just leave without telling me
and then she broke it to me,

"Susie was raped."

I didn't fully understand the meaning of rape,

I was only 10yrs old.

Eight years passed and every day I wished I was there for her,

my best friend,

a victim of one of the cruelest crimes.

My best friend,

every night I hear her scream for help,
it got so bad that I started blaming myself for not being there to
stand up for her.

My best friend,

raped on the night of her birthday.

My best friend forced to spread her legs and take the pain.

My best friend every sense of happiness beaten out of her that
night.

I tried to stop thinking of it,
but every time I did, she came back into my thoughts
I tried to replay images of when she and I were on the playground
having fun,
but all I could see was her face shooting out tears.

So Susie

my best friend

I apologize,
I wish I could've gone back in time and been there for you.
I'm sorry,
I dedicate this poem to you and for all the victims of this devilish
crime, known as rape.

You are my hero,
I can't imagine the pain you went through,
but I wanted to let you know that we'll get through this
you're not alone.
They say things happen for a reason,
I couldn't find an answer but I know if we all work together
we can stop this.

Peter Santos

16
St. Paul Christian Academy

Influences:
Poets like Tupac Shakur made rhyming my choice of style.

Why I write:
I started writing Poetry in late 2008, but I've always liked it growing up. My poem is titled "One Beautiful Crime." It is sort of an "anthem" for all graffiti writers, but it is also a quick glimpse of the graffiti culture.

Pete Santos

Beautiful Crime

IT'S BEEN AROUND SINCE THE BEGINNING OF TIME,
BACK THEN IT WAS LEGAL BUT TODAY IT'S A CRIME.
GRAFFITI HAS BEEN AROUND FOREVER,
SINCE CAVEMEN WROTE ON WALLS TO KMART'S
BATHROOM STALLS
GRAFFITI IS AND HAS BEEN HISTORY,
WITHOUT IT, IT WOULD BE A MYSTERY AS TO WHO
WAS HERE AND THERE.
BUT IT IS STILL A CRIME?!!
SIGNED NAMES ON A WALL ARE NOW A THOUSAND
DOLLAR FINE,
TELL ME HOW THAT IS JUSTICE
GIVE ME AN EXPLANATION,
ALL I'M DOING HERE IS **URBAN BEAUTIFICATION**,
ADDING COLOR TO OUR ISLAND AND BRINGING BACK
THE LIFE
BUT THEY STILL SAY WE CAUSE THE UNNECESSARY
STRIFE.
TELL ME HOW CAN YOU VANDALIZE A WALL
COVERED WITH MOLD,
OLD PAINT IS CHIPPING AND IT LOOKS LIKE NO ONE
CARES
BUT WE STILL ACKNOWLEDGE THE FACT THAT IT IS
A BLANK CANVAS AND STILL STATE THAT WE WERE
THERE.
GRAFFITI HAS SAVED MY LIFE IN MANY DIFFERENT
WAYS

From providing me with a passion
To saying no to Mary Jane.
 It has altered my perception and my view on
the world,
Hurled pigments that aligned like the body of
a beautiful girl.
So if you think graffiti writers are no-good
kids out to destroy Guam
Well
      Wrong,
          Wrong,
            Wrong,
That's wrong times three.
An example of a graff writer is portrayed by
me.
Well what can I say I go to church everyday.
Yes that's true but wait, there's more,
I got skin as white as the sand on the shores,
I do my chores,
Plus no pimples so that means I got some
clean pores.
With that being said it shows that I'm not that
wild,
I got good moral ethics and in fact I'm a
pretty decent child.
But don't get me wrong all graff writers
aren't the same
Some do it for the love of the art
Some do it for the fame,
Others do it for pure destruction because
they're mad at the world,
Failing in school ,

No job and broken up with their girls.
So I can't lie graffiti ain't all nice,
it's a mixture of the good and the bad,
mad kids who are not fully understood wish
they could have a release in life
something to get their minds off things
and are comforted by the meditation that
graffiti brings.
Look through the eyes of a writer and it's an
experience like no other,
you view life in Krylon and Belton colors.
A little middle shock blue and hint of poison
green,
mix 'em both together and it's a beautiful
thing.
Blended colors like a fruit smoothie
straight from the buzz.
And a force field of mismatched colors just
because.
Graffiti knows no limits
adopted by both rich and the poor.
Their music ranges from "CAN I KICK IT?"
to "LOVE SONG" by the Cure.
By now you can see that, graffiti transcends
all boundaries and breaks all the rules,
fools claim it's vandalism, but it's more than
that,
we paint our names in more than just white
and black.
Pack mops markers and cans with all your
different caps
and for a quick hit you gotta carry your

Necessary slaps.
Get up,
    Get up
        then **Get Up** some more.
Keep your finger pressed on a fat cap 'til it
gets sore.
Experience the rush of a marker to a wall,
Remember snitches get stitches and that's
what leads to your downfall.
Paint spitting out of an NY Fat is my visual
high,
Creating a flared handstyle with a can of
            KRYYYYYYYYYYYLON,
Everyday getting your
            STYYYYYYYYYYYLe ON.
With different caps that create different
sizes
That hypnotizes the writer who forever de-
spises the man,
Whose plan is their keep us down.
Their thick layers of paint prevent our names
to be found.
But no matter what they do they will continue
to fail,
Because us graffiti writers will continue to
prevail.

So if you listen to this poem line after line,
You'll find graffiti to be one

BEAUTIFUL CRIME.

John Norman Sarmiento

19yrs old
University of Guam, JFK Graduate

Influences:
Mrs. Reglos, family, other poets,
society, women

Why I write:
I've learned growing up that the power of the word is not one to be stifled. Some of the most influential individuals in the world managed to reach thousands with their writing, whether it was through essays, novels, short stories, prose, or poetry; because of that I choose to write. I've always dreamed of leaving a positive impact on society—more specifically on Guam—and one of the ways I believe I can do it is through literature. Although I know that in most cases a pen cannot be any mightier than a sword, an idea can outlast the strongest type of steel.

JOHN SARMIENTO

Arctic

I was told to call him Uncle
Only 5 yrs older than me, so close I felt like I should have called
him brother instead
but I called him Arctic because he was so cool and just as
unpredictable as the sea
I remember one night, we floated beneath the sky
He told me of all the lies he's used to get by in life hoping I wouldn't
need them

That night he told me that God was a sniper
Heaven was his vantage point, stars were empty bullet casings
That God was shooting beauty hoping we'd all be able to speak
angel one day
My uncle never figured that my poetry wasn't the language used to
get through the Golden Gates
but I think he did figure
that stars pinned on a night blue Marine Corps uniform would
allow him to play God

The day he signed his life away I decided to uncross the T and
un-dot the I
Arctic
I didn't think it was cool for him to leave me and I still wish he was
a little more predictable
Now he's a full-fledged sniper, the only sure shot in my family
Hands so steady he carries the livelihood of platoons on his
fingertips
but when he marches home to his family, no one recognizes
him — no one talks to him
He's as hollow as a bullet tip
A 7.62mm American Dream
His soul is a standard issue M40A1 loaded with top secret missions
he's not allowed to tell me about
All he knows is military protocol and he acts like I can't understand
them

but it's so simple to understand silence

But when he sleeps that silence is broken
and I understand his top secrets through his screams
Maybe playing God is every man's dream
My uncle takes forks in the road, bends them into crosshairs for his
sniping scope
He fulfills destinies
Lays men, women, and children to rest at bullet speeds
And I still wonder, "when does a man decide to take lives for a
living?"
I'm not here to bag on the military, I'm just looking for a lifesaver
to throw to my uncle
He is drowning in regret for choosing to become a bringer-of-death
He is Arctic
Flashbacks of headshots make him sweat ice cold
He sleeps in his own sea
Eyes like icebergs, 80% open
He's always just 20% asleep
Too afraid to face ghosts in his dreams

I wish he would have realized
that bullets leave holes in more places than in a victim's body
and in the target rings of a complete family he's become the bull's
eye that we are missing

We no longer share stories
I guess his teenage years are at ease in Military profile folders
no longer close enough to call him my brother
but he's taught me well, told me of all the lies he's used to get by in
life
So on his last visit, when he asked, "Do you still love me?"
I told him,
"Arctic, no matter how cold you get
I will always love the sea."

JOHN SARMIENTO

Gerber Daisy

I remember when it was hard for me to move my feet
My heart was pollinated heavily with bad ideas about how life
should be
that I was weighed down to the ground
in a field filled with weeds
with the potential to blossom in every dying heart beat
but I never did
I needed the buzz from a sincere Queen Honeybee
then you buzzed on by
My patterns were designed to play hide and seek with the sunlight
that shined from your smile and from your eyes
I was just another weed in the darkness of a field 'til you picked me up
into the light, counted to 15

and helped me blossom into a **Gerber** Daisy

And you began to pick the lines of my poetry like they were petals

Kicking your feet, hanging from a high-rise in a **Sim**city colored like
flower filled meadows
And every petal read the same line:
I love you, and I'm never gonna stop
I love you, and I'm never gonna stop
I love you, and I'm never gonna stop

I let you carry me because you promised that you would, carefully
With my flower face sitting in the palm of your hand, you picked
I let you pick,
but in the end you picked to leave me

To join your shining, smiling eyes with the air in the **G**olden **S**tate
Left me back in Guam soil for someone else to take

I never knew a Queen bee could make such a mistake
And for a while my ideas about you lay scattered
hidden in dark places like the catacombs in a bee hive
I was the dying weed you helped re-root back into life
And I refuse to regress from the light
You taught me with the beat of your wings how to grow under the
most tremendous forms of adversity

And I got my roots crossed, hoping that the wind sweeps me up, back
onto my feet
I hope it paints a mural with these flower petals so the whole world
may see
That maybe a Queen bee doesn't need a flower, she needs a king
So I hope you find yours
But know that his wings can never be picked like the lines of my
poetry
And here, perhaps destined to stay, my final petal reads:
I love you, but not in the same way

JOHN SARMIENTO

Grand Piano

They laid you in the 15th room down the hall to the right
Away from the bustle of a busy hospital
As if you could hear the noise in your comma

And even after visiting hours, I manage to stay by your bedside
by sending you these notes I play on this grand piano
They tell me it was donated by a retired doctor
Right now Hope is my physician and I'm just one more in the
group of patience
in the waiting room

I realize now that jealousy isn't all bad, it's another incentive for
you to live
Don't you know there are tons of girls wanting to fill the empty
space you left in my heart?
But my heart's locked, its locks are shaped like music notes
and you're my inspiration to play with these keys

I never took piano lessons but you always said the hardest thing
anyone could teach is to listen
and I learned how to do that on my own
You joked that the insides of my ears were shaped like treble and
bass clefs
And tonight, all I'm hearing are your vital signs
So to make sure you don't flat line, I'm playing nothing but the
sharp notes

I jumped on a plane from Guam to California the moment I got
a call that you were hurt
I already lost you once to the complications of a long
distance relationship
And I refuse to lose you to the complications of a speeding
accident
I always told you to slow down, and I thought you understood

that a melody played in moderato allows you to hear its beauty, same with a scenic route, you miss the breath-taking scenery when you voluntarily blur them out

But it's no secret, it's clear you're an angelic, speed demon, and I'm just a slam poetry/music junkie
Except you were taught to read the road signs and you understand the speed limit
I'm still trying to figure out how these metaphors find me
I can't read notes, all I can read are the titles at the tops of these music sheets
This one reads *I Need You*, that one reads *Melodies of Life*
But not even Hope can accept them as prescriptions for a dose of Miracle to save you

I wish I could read notes, I wish I could replace your veins with these piano strings
So in case your heart weakens I can play *Melodies of Life* to keep it beating
So I could play *I Need You* to strengthen its pumping
I wish I could jam these sustain pedals to keep your soul from departing

We already broke up a while back, let's not break the last string of connection we have left
I need you to fight, because even being this far from our break up night
I know you remember the song we both agreed to compose together,
titled: *Our Future*

Jewelry

My parents had scepters made of metal and wood
that shined like gold and silver under the hot sun when they
tended the fields
They knew how to bow and how to kneel because planting
rice made them experts
They knew how to save and how to appreciate because being
poor made them professionals
My parents left their homeland in search of a better life and
found their way here
I'm their every incarnation of their every hope and dream
Forget sterling silver or white gold because they've got a
walking, breathing piece
But they don't see the dilemma that they've put me in

I'm in a push and a pull between my cultural identity
My mom always said that I was born and raised on Guam but
I'm really from the Philippines
I guess that means I'm supposed to be part F.O.B. and part
almost-chad
I'm supposed to be able to sing:
Bayang magiliw,
Perlas ng Silanganan,
Alab ng puso,
Sa dibdib mo'y buhay
And have an English translation but I don't, because I don't
know enough to translate it
but I know that somewhere in there, that Philippine National
Anthem talks about pride
Something I'm supposed to have:
I was born full Filipino, but now I'm half American Colonized

I can't be proud of my heritage
I know virtually nothing about the first half of it
and the second half, I know so much about, that sometimes

I'm ashamed of it
I know exactly what it means to be American Colonized
It means that Uncle Sam wanted them to force this island's
native culture to its knees and now he wants **YOU** to load and
point a M16 but he gets to call all the shots
It means being an Unincorporated Territory **OCCUPIED** by
the United States of America and still called "**FREE**"

For too long I've searched for what it means to be a direct
descendant of the Philippines
I've chewed and swallowed every sharp Tagalog word that I
could expecting some sort of meaning to crawl up from deep
inside of me - - words like *Salita*, *Tayo*, at *Laban* - -Speak,
Stand, and Fight!
I shut my eyes tightly, let my subconscious be the projector
with the insides of my eyelids as the projector screens
I figured there'd have to be some sort of cultural identity
embedded within my dreams!
But I was wrong
And so now I fear that in the future my own children will not
know their culture
they'll be spitting images of their father who snipped off his
native tongue for unified slurs, who blotted out the Sun and
replaced it with Stars and Stripes, who defines Filipino as
hard working but never worked as hard as his parents ever
did a day in his life
I would HATE for my children to be exactly like me 'cause
I'm just my parents' walking, breathing, paradoxical piece of
Jewelry.

Teacher, Teacher

When I was younger
teachers over emphasized the need for me to raise my hand
before speaking
or before giving an answer
I never really minded because I knew it was a rule I HAD to
follow
or else my parents would be called
I was always that kid shooting his hand up faster than teachers
could ever finish questions

But at some point I began to feel like raising my hand was just
another tool the system was using to mechanize me
So whenever I felt brave enough I'd ask a teacher,
"Ms., explain to me why we have to raise our hand again?"
"BECAUSE! IT'S A RULE, JOHNNY!"

But now that I'm older, I see things a lot differently
In the future, when I'm a teacher
And I get a wisecrack, just as brave enough as me, asking,
"Mr. Sarmiento? You didn't write it on the list of rules on the wall.
So, why do we HAVE to raise our hands again?"
I'll say, **"Because! every answer you formulate,
every opinion you create in your head, every
sort of response that I get...
is your step closer to reaching those stars, it's
your step closer to success and you should be
proud of it!
That's why I require you to raise your hand."**

Whatever happened to teaching kids about creativity,
expression, and individuality?

We've bubble wrapped them in uniforms and labeled them like
products with more acronyms than poets could ever come up
with
Like **E.S.L.   L.D.   M.R.   &   S.P.ED.**
But somehow everything remains okay
I guess it's 'cause we've taught these kids
to look at themselves as products of society anyway!

We stuck them in **D.I.**
DIRECT INSTRUCTION classes, posed them with questions and
required them to give the same answer over and over again in
unison, like records
How do we expect them not to be skipping when we treat them
like they're already broken
The only time they can respond
is at the **click** of a *clicker* or the **snap** of a *finger*

"Is your reading getting any better?"

ready and **click**

"No."

"Is your reading getting any better?"

ready and **snap**

"No."

We force them to tuck in their shirts like treat-less, groomed
dogs
and mechanize them like cultural robots
But yet here I am, Scout's honor
I promise to implement **D.I.** in my class— **Distinct
Individuality**
and you can bet I'll teach it enthusiastically

I won't write kids off as thorns from roses and group 'em up
'cause then all we'd have are pricks and a less educated society
left to bleed

Maybe I don't have the credentials to be busting anybody's
chops here
But I've carved enough credit into my bones
to know exactly the type of teacher I am going to be
I'll teach my students the basics of reading and
writing,

but most importantly

I'll teach my students how to speak

Jessie Rae C. Tedtaotao

18 yrs old
Pulantat, Yoña
Southern High graduate

Influences:

My mom, my father, people who face life's struggles, the colonization and mistreatment of Guåhån and many other homes, and all those who support my writing.

Why I write:

Writing started off as a therapeutic thing for me. It was the only thing I could turn to, to be heard and understood. But now, it also plays a part in how I am able to express myself to others, connect with the world around me, share my stories, and send messages to those willing to listen. It gives me the opportu- nity to voice my opinions on the issues we face. I write because it is the one thing that makes a difference in my life, and the lives of others.

Jessie Rae Tedtaotao

Barricade of Broken Dreams

WHAT EVER HAPPENED TO US...
BACK WHEN WE WERE KIDS WE WOULD BRING ALL THE CHAIRS TO THE CORNER
USE THEM TO MAKE A BARRICADE,
BLOCK THE WORLD OUT....AND PLAY GROWN-UP
WE ALWAYS IMAGINED OUR DREAM HOMES BUILT RIGHT NEXT TO EACH OTHER,
THE ONLY THING SEPARATING US WAS AN AVOCADO TREE THAT BENT INTO THE SHAPE OF OUR TREE HOUSE
AND OUR BIKES WERE THE BEST SUVs HORNET SPORTING GOODS COULD EVER SELL,
IT WAS A ONE-SEAT VEHICLE THAT PACKED ALL OUR DREAMS
I WANT TO GO BACK TO WHEN THE ONLY TIME I LIED
WAS SO THAT GRANDMA WOULD NEVER FIND OUT THAT WE NEVER ACTUALLY SLEPT DURING NAP TIME..
THERE WERE TIMES THAT WE FOUGHT BECAUSE THEY ONLY HAD ONE BAT, AND I HATED BEING THE PITCHER...
YOU ALWAYS SET UP HIDE-AND-SEEK, SO THAT I WOULD BE THE IT...
AND SOMETIMES, I WOULD BUY A PACK OF SKITTLES BECAUSE I KNEW YOU LIKED THAT CANDY,
AND JUST TO MAKE YOU MAD..I WOULDN'T SHARE WITH YOU...
WHAT EVER HAPPENED TO US...
NOW THAT WE'RE OLDER, THE CHAIRS SEEM TO BE MISSING, OUR BARRICADE IS BROKEN...
THE WORLD HAS COME IN...
AND THIS GROWN-UP THING..IS NOT PRETEND ANYMORE..
YOUR DREAM HOME IS NOWHERE NEXT TO MINE, IT'S NOT EVEN BUILT ON THIS ISLAND..
AND THE ONE THING THAT SEPARATES US
IS THAT SHINY NEW NAME TAG THAT SAYS U.S. AIR FORCE..
YOU SAID YOU WERE COMING HOME TO VISIT
I WISH YOU WERE COMING HOME TO STAY
I HAVE TO BE PROUD OF YOU...YOU KNEW EXACTLY WHAT YOU WANTED AND YOU WENT OUT AND GOT IT...

I ALWAYS KNEW YOU WEREN'T A QUITTER..
WHEN YOU TOLD ME YOU WERE GOING TO JOIN THE MILITARY,
I TRIED TO TALK YOU OUT OF IT, BUT YOUR MIND WAS ALREADY SET...
WHO WOULD HAVE THOUGHT THAT LIVING YOUR DREAM WOULD MEAN ME LIVING MY NIGHTMARE,
YOUR VISIT WAS CANCELLED..BECAUSE THEY CALLED YOU TO IRAQ
CAN THIS GET ANY WORSE?
YOUR DEPLOYMENT IS SET ON PLAY
YOUR VISITS PUT ON PAUSE
AND MY MIND IS
STUCK ON REWIND...
I HATE TO KEEP FOCUSING ON THE PAST, BUT I CANT HELP IT..
THAT'S THE ONLY PLACE WHERE I CAN SEE YOU...
NOW, YOUR FACE IS MY COMPUTER SCREEN...
OUR LAUGHS ARE INSTANT MESSAGES (LOL)
AND OUR SECRET HANDSHAKE IS 'SCROLL DOWN' AND 'RIGHT CLICK'...
I WISH YOU HAD NEVER JOINED THE AIR FORCE
FORGIVE ME FOR BEING SELFISH, I JUST WANT MY COUSIN BACK...
MY CHILDHOOD MEMORY, MY PARTNER IN CRIME, I JUST WANT TO PLAY PRETEND AGAIN...
THESE DAYS..I GO OUTSIDE AND ALL I HEAR IS SILENCE...
THAT AVOCADO TREE IS STILL BENT, BUT I DON'T SEE THE TREE HOUSE ANYMORE..
I SWEAR.. I'LL PITCH YOU THE BALL, JUST PROMISE ME YOU'LL HIT IT AND RUN HOME,
I'LL BE IT FOR AS LONG AS YOU WANT, JUST PROMISE ME I'LL BE ABLE TO FIND YOU...
I'LL BUY A PACK OF SKITTLES, JUST PROMISE THAT WHEN I OPEN IT..YOU'LL BE THERE SO I CAN SHARE IT WITH YOU...

WHAT EVER HAPPENED TO US..

WHAT EVER HAPPENED TO OUR BARRICADE

Jessie Rae Tedtaotao

Childhood

i am a child who misses her mom
every time she goes in and out to
two jobs just to keep us above the poverty
line.

i am a child who watches on the side
as the soldiers carry her daddy to his burial
site
had to compete with the world to
either win him as a dad or lose him as a hero

i am a child who can't have
family road trips with no destination
because gas prices set limitations

i am a child who has more sense than you
saved up in a jar because
i am afraid that my household's income
will set my future's outcome

i am a child who wastes her time
spilling herself out on MySpace
because trying to make you understand
will take so much longer

i am a child who is protected by an act
that claims "no child is left behind"
but how can i be left behind
when the world is just standing still?
we're all stuck on suggesting how the
world should be progressing but no actual
action
is being taken, so for now, we are all just
linking
and forming this one big circle, standing in
place

i am a child who walks away, voluntarily,

when grown-ups are talking
because adult conversations are just
too much frustration
and you may think that i am too young to
understand all of this
but let me tell you
when you're wide awake, i'm watching Barney &
Friends
but when you fall fast asleep, I switch to CNN
because I understand everything
but watching you and your kind
makes me a child, afraid to grow up

Jessie Rae Teotaotao

A Change Made for HER

I never realized how beautiful she really was
until I saw her tears, one day, being clogged up
by trash covering a drain.
It was at that moment I knew
it was my duty to bend down
and clear the path for her pain to flow.
But right when i removed the blockage,
her tears increased
and started gushing through the drain
and it made me wonder,
"if I cleared the mess then why was she still crying?"
Then it came to me, cleaning up the trash
only made a difference, it didnt make a change,
and a change is what we need.
A change is what will make her pain stop.
See i used to be a litter bug.
Trash cans were always too far,
recycling was always too much work,
and my papers were always useless
with even just a tiny drop of ink.
But now I've changed my ways.
My trash cans are in my pockets,
recycling is a daily practice and
my papers are soaked with
so much ink they make my pens feel jealous.
It took her tears to flow for me to
realize that she is Mother Earth,
mothering all of us and she will always love us.
As much as we mistreat her she will
always take care of us, but just like our real moms
there is only so much she can bear.
Only so much she can take and

we take a lot more from her.
But what happens when there's nothing left?
What happens when she is burned down, polluted,
cut to pieces and destroyed...
What happens when Mother Earth is dead?
See, we always need her, but
now she needs us. This is our time to
come together as one,
to reshape the recycling triangle into
a circle of helping hands, to stop thinking
of just ourselves and start thinking green,
to reduce, reuse and remind the others to do the same
because once we open our eyes and
change our ways of living, we will all see
just how beautiful Mother Earth really is.

Jessie Rae Tedtaotao

Virgin Invasion

I lost my innocence a long time a ago
and i wish i could get it back
my strength was weakened
couldn't push your muscles off of me
your hands held my wrists down
and your legs pinned my thighs to the ground
and your breath clogged up my lungs so
i couldn't scream the word "no!" and "stop!"
or "get your filthy self off me.."
i was only breathing silence
i am treated as one of your skanks, your concubines
and i've been passed around and invaded by
your enemies and now..
i stare with shame at the land i walk on
because i am no longer indigenous to my own home
i am a walking historic site
of who has come and gone
as if i was some sort of friend-with-benefits
but the only one benefiting from all of it
was you..i hold in my veins the blood
of the ones i turned my backs to
i can't say i am full chamoru
because i know that my island has been run too long
by foreigners
whose semen is running somewhere in my system
i hide the truth with lies that make the pain pause
but never come to a complete stop
you love the look of fear in my eyes
the look of confusion of who i really am

you love the orgasm you get from
taking what is mine and claiming it as yours
you cut wounds in my skin..and filled them with
your image of progress and stitch them up with
your sharp lies and then
you wrap it with band aids made from
colonization and now though my cuts have healed
my scars are still there
the memory is still there and all i want is to
hit my head so hard and cause myself
memory loss so that the image of you raping my people can
fade away and never come back
now i am occupied by a country that doesnt even know i exist
and i am forced to pledge to the red white and blue
as weak as i am..as confused as i look..i still stand in
front of their flag with my palms dripping red blood
with arms that are filled with black and blue bruises
and stare into the white of their lies but the only thing i see
is the memory of that day in 1521, the day all of this
started, the day i can't get rid of...

the day you took my innocence..

Jessie Rae Tedtaotao

The Blame Game

They asked me...what made me so angry
and i said..**THEM**
the ones who tie-dyed our culture with westernization
THEM
the ones who hold me hostage in my own home
THEM
the ones who say i am free but still oppressed by
THEM
THEM is what made me so angry
but see...just because anger is all you're seeing
doesn't mean that's all that's there..
further down inside...covered up by the anger is death
yes...i am dying..and they asked me
well what is killing you..
and i said..
US
the ones who are letting **THEM** get away this
US
the ones who are playing dead just because playing alive is so
much harder
US
the ones who raise our flag beneath the red, white, and blue
US
the ones who turn our cheeks to the damage they are causing
US
US is what is killing me..but see..death is a battle field
and and on that field are two forces fighting..
and then they asked..well who is fighting
and i said

ME
the one who wont give in to all the fingers pointing at
ME
the one who stands up for what she believes in
ME
the one who'd rather raise her fist then cover up her heart
ME is who is fighting..and i wont give up until
THEM and **US** stop playing this ridiculous blame game
stop pointing your fingers, instead
open them up and offer a helping hand
because the world will be unbalanced without **THEM**
and **US**.
It's like having problems but no solutions, questions but no
answers, it's like having trouble but no help
stop drawing this line between **THEM** and **US**
because it is not getting **US** anywhere..
just more people dying
and more children crying and soon
there will be nothing but silence...because
THEM against **US** will have caused
every soul that was breathing
every heart that was beating
every child that was dreaming
to disappear
all of that will be gone
and in that silence
it will be **ME** who is standing there
saying..
"I told **YOU** so!"

Jessie Rae Tedtaotao

UNCLE SAM'S INTERROGATION

WHO GOES TO WAR TO DEFEND HIS LAND?

"IT IS NOT I," SAYS UNCLE SAM

WHO HAS THE BLOOD OF SOLDIERS IN THE PALM OF HIS HAND?

"IT IS NOT I," SAYS UNCLE SAM

WHO LEAVES THEIR FAMILY TO DECREASE HUMANITY?

WHO FOLLOWS ORDERS AND CROSSES BORDERS?

WHO TAKES COMMANDS TO ENTER OTHER PEOPLES' LAND?

WHO GETS PAID TO FOLLOW THE WAYS OF THE "ALL-AMERICAN DREAMER"?

WHOSE FINGER PULLED THE TRIGGER, JUST TO TAKE A LIFE?

WHO HAD TO LEAVE THEIR PREGNANT WIFE?

WHO IS OUT THERE PRETENDING THAT THIS WAR IS DEFENDING?

(BUT REALLY THEY BELIEVE U.S. TROOPS SHOULD JUST LEAVE IRAQ AND THE OTHERS ALONE)

WHO ARE THE SOLDIERS LONGING FOR THEIR HOME?

WHO HAS THE GUILT OF KILLING RUNNING THROUGH THEIR MINDS?

WHO FOLLOWS THE MOTTO OF NOT LEAVING A MAN BEHIND?

WHO KNOWS THAT THE PLEDGE SAYS "JUSTICE FOR ALL"?

Jessie Rae Tedtaotao

WHO READS IN OUR NEWSPAPERS "ANOTHER SON OF GUAM FALLS"?

WHO HAS TO SALUTE THE AMERICAN FLAG?

WHO IS THAT LITTLE GIRL THAT JUST LOST HER DAD?

WHO BELONGS TO THOSE HANDS THAT JUST DROPPED THAT BOMB?

WHO ARE THE CHILDREN MISSING THEIR MOMS?

WHO HAS TO GRIEVE AND BURY A FAMILY MAN?

"IT IS NOT I," SAYS UNCLE SAM...........

BUT WHO RECRUITS THESE TROOPS AND PUTS THESE SOLDIERS IN BOOTS?

WHO HELD UP A MONKEY SAYING, "THIS IS GUAM"?...

(HAS THOSE SAME MONKEYS LOADING HIS GUNS, HAS THOSE SAME MONKEYS DROPPING HIS BOMBS

LIKE THAT WILL MAKE 'EM WORTHY OF BEING CALLED HIS SONS)

WHO CAN REVEAL THAT HIS FREEDOM'S NOT REAL AND THAT HE'S GREEDY FOR POWER BY WANTING LAND BY THE HOUR?

WHO CAN'T ACCEPT OTHER CULTURAL WAYS AND JUST LET THEM BE?

"YES!" SAYS UNCLE SAM, "NOW THAT'D BE ME!"

Jessie Rae Tedtaotao

A Daughter's Addiction

i was always ashamed of telling people that
i didn't have that best friend, going shopping with, telling secrets
to type-of-bond with you.
but i've come to realize that this is what makes my love for you so
special.
because even though we have those arguments and
disagreements,
i still wake up loving you
i still go to bed loving you
i still live to tell you "i love you."
all my life i've tried to find things to do to make you proud
turning away smoking and skipping and drinking
picking my friends based on how you would feel about them
but it has just put me in a deeper hole screaming for you to listen
begging for you to reach out and accept me
for me
no one in our family ever took an interest in poetry like i do, so i
understand why this confuses you.
but MOM,
this is me,
this is who i am
and i've come to accept it
because not too long ago someone told me that i couldn't keep
this passion inside me,
locked up in isolation that appears as a body to the human eye

Jessie Rae Tedtaotao

i know this is not the ideal dream you had in mind for me
which is why i've been running from it
but i gotta stop because until i take pride in what i do
you can never take pride in it yourself
so i invite you to other half of my life
to have you sit here and witness the greatness that comes from
within me
i would like to tell you and the whole world why i write
my reasons are simple......
writing is more than just a hobby to me.
writing saved my life. it's what keeps me out of trouble
it's what keeps my head right, my chin up, my chest out,
it's what took my hand from over my heart, formed it into a fist and
threw it up in the air
writing is what made me forgive my father.
it's what helped me through the pain and the grief of losing my
grandparents
writing is my gravity, pulling my head out of the clouds and holding
me in place on this earth
i have a hard time telling people how i feel
but for some reason once my hand grips that pen
there is no hesitation to write exactly what is on my mind
and my mind has a tendency to push words out of my mouth,
not thinking twice about what they mean or how they make people
feel,
but when I'm writing, i have the chance to oversee what i am trying
to say and change it if there's any doubt that it wouldn't be heard
or understood the way i want it to.
writing is my circle of trust
trusting the paper to never betray me,

Jessie Rae Tedtaotao

trusting the pen to never judge me,
trusting the mic to never take my words and twist them around
and in return they trust me to never give up on them.
writing is my fairytale, where it doesn't always have to end with
everybody living happily ever after
but at least it considers my thoughts and my feelings
writing is my heart, poetry is my passion,
and the blood that is flowing through my veins is, in actuality,
words trying to escape into society, which makes spoken word my
voice.
and even though this mic scares me to death every time i step up
to it,
what keeps me coming back
is the feeling that takes over when i'm done reciting my pieces.
the feeling of accomplishment,
the feeling of relief,
the feeling of being heard.
writing is my drug
and it has built into an addiction so bad that it has come between
me and you.
and it has hurt you so deep i feel like you're intimidated by it
but MOM
please do not feel like you are losing me, because i am only trying
to find myself
and i can only do that through my writing
so as hard as it is to understand and as hard as it is to accept,
i ask you to please not give up on me
because this is who i am
this is what interests me
and i can never change that

and i don't care if it doesn't get me on t.v.

i don't care if it doesn't get me the nicest black lexus, tinted full face, with spinners on all four tires

i don't care if it takes me to the life of the hungry and the homeless

because in the end i'll know that i am doing what i was born to do and that will always make me happy

MOM

please do not level yourself with my writing

you will always be first in my eyes,

in my mind,

in my heart,

you will always be first in my life

because YOU are my writing!

Jessie Rae Tedtaotao

the I in erIc

thursday march 19th
i followed my sister to mt. carmel
to drop her kids off
and as she spoke to the teacher
my niece *pulled* me to the carpet
where her classmates were playing
one by one, they introduced themselves
his name is erIc and right after the other two
told me their names he came out of nowhere
and decided to D
           R
          O
               P a bomb in my face to start my day
he said, " i've never seen my father."
my jaw dropped, my knees got weak
and i wasn't just sweating bullets, i was sweating guns that were
loaded and ready to be fired.
i swear i had never met this kid in my life,
but i felt like i knew so much about him
where he was coming from, where he was at, and where he was
headed
i saw more of me in his eyes than i ever saw in the mirror
i got up from the carpet and walked away
stared at the walls that were
covered with drawings and expressions of toddlers..
but my mind was stuck on that 2 second conversation..
my eyes filled with tears and as hard as i was trying to
hold them back, they started sprinting d
                            o
                            w
                            n my face...
i never went back to talk to him.
i was so mixed in my emotions
 pissed that his father could leave him

and scared.
i was scared of how brave he was..
this little boy had so much strength to reveal
something that took me years to accept..
after we left mt. carmel, I tried so hard to put the incident
behind me, but I couldn't
it just kept *running* through my mind

i could have said something to make a difference
in his life.
i could have given him the heads up
on how the world would turn differently
because he was lacking a dad..
i could have given him a hug, a hand shake, some kind of gesture that showed him
that we had similarities,
because i was once just like him..
i could have done something..
but instead, i replayed the image of both our fathers, and just walked away.
and it made me understand how easy it was for them to abandon us,
because sometimes fear overpowers love, and it's scary when you don't know how to show it.
they walked away from us because leaving someone alone is easier than hearing them say that they need you.
so i get it..
i walked away from you thinking i didn't know how to help you
because I was afraid that i was the only one who could,
and it was something I wasn't ready to admit.
but now,
all i feel is regret.
all i have is the thought of how i had someone there to help me beat
life at its own game.
my heart is filled with pain
and it pushed me to grab a pen and write something...
so erIc, this poem is for you.
i would like to tell you that i hated my father for leaving me..
and it took me years to forgive him
but i hope you can do it quicker, because with hate comes anger
and nobody deserves to live their *child*hood angry..

you need to know that there is a difference between a father and
a dad.
a father helps to make you,
while a dad helps you make it
a dad is an image that can be painted in anybody you feel deserves
that title
i painted mine in my grandpa.
as you grow older you will find that the world has a way of
reminding you that your father is gone.
it will rub it in your face
with father's day cards
and christmas presents
and all of your upcoming birthdays
but do not let that get to you
instead pick up a pen and write
get a paint brush and paint
grab a spray can and mark your presence..
break out a dance move and dance like there
is lava beneath your feet
pick up a mic and speak
because these things allow you to express yourself
and expression is the best prescription of pain killers
know that to struggle means: *to make strenuous or great efforts in the face
of difficulties*,
so struggling is nothing to be ashamed of.
i can't promise you that it's going to be easy,
but i can guarantee that along the way
you will find people, like i did, who will care about you
and be there for you
to en**courage** you and to pick you up when you *fall*...
to take the moon and the stars and tattoo them
to the inside of your eyelids so that you can always close your eyes
and dream...
you will have people who will be there for you when you feel
happy, sad, pissed, alone, scared, and even when you can't feel at all...
these people will be more of a family to you than your father
could ever be....they will be there to help you push yourself..
and one day...you will be successful
because you made it through life. through all the hard times and
set backs

you pulled yourself through
and at that point, though you have never seen your father
i will bet my life,

that he will be dying to see you

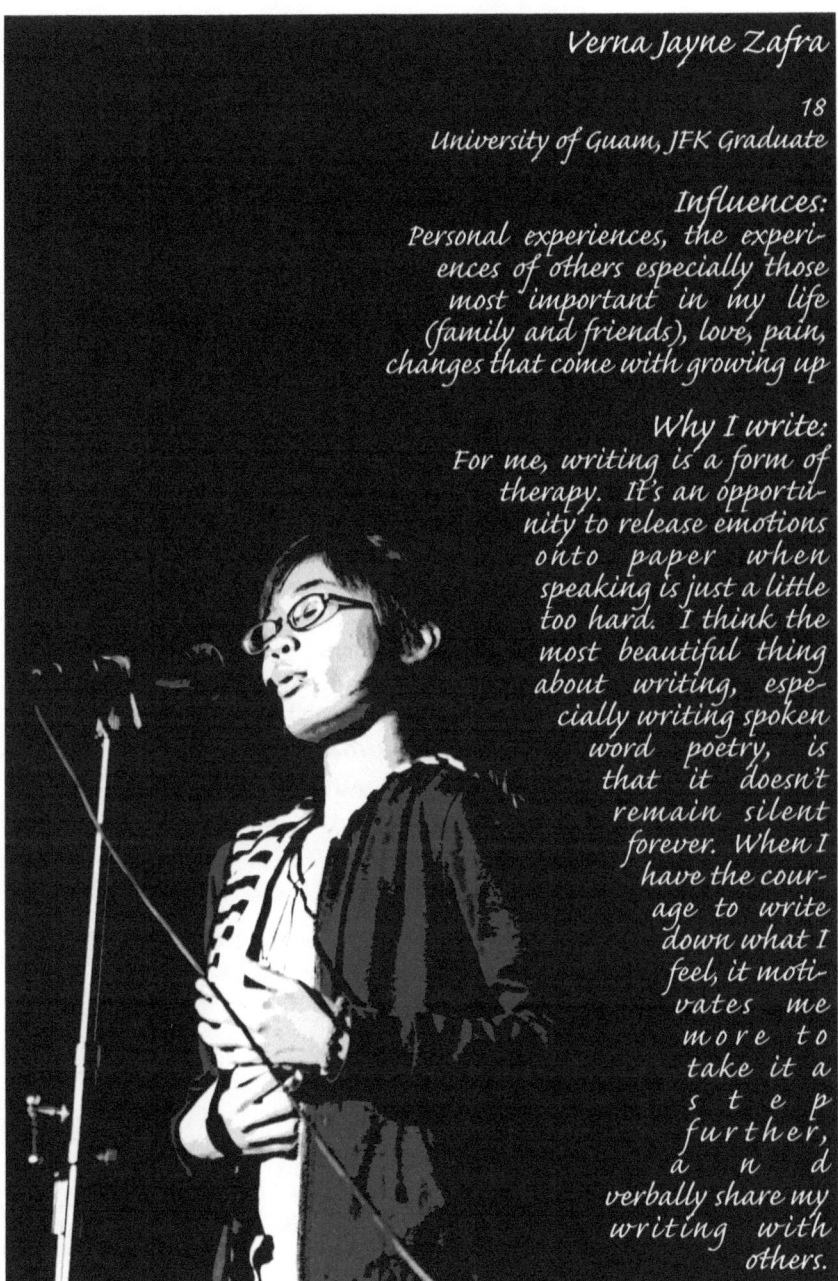

Verna Jayne Zafra

18
University of Guam, JFK Graduate

Influences:
Personal experiences, the experiences of others especially those most important in my life (family and friends), love, pain, changes that come with growing up

Why I write:
For me, writing is a form of therapy. It's an opportunity to release emotions onto paper when speaking is just a little too hard. I think the most beautiful thing about writing, especially writing spoken word poetry, is that it doesn't remain silent forever. When I have the courage to write down what I feel, it motivates me more to take it a step further, and verbally share my writing with others.

Verna Zafra

ARTWORK

Some people say that Love has a way with words,
That sweet verses and clever rhymes are all you need
To communicate with the heart ❤.
They say when it comes to romance,
Poetry beats out Art
And Poets are more romantic than Artists could ever be.
And maybe it's true,
Because I Am a Poet
(And I am pretty freakin' romantic!)
But you see, Poets are Artists too.
So for a little while,
Let me replace my *pen* with a *brush*
And my *paper* with *canvas*
So I can attempt to paint
A perfect picture of Me and You.
I'll be contemporary with an old school touch,
Fuse abstract with concrete
To portray the many ways that you have changed my world.
I'll spread your **PASSIONATE REDS** and *soulful blues*
Into the dull corners of my **black** and **white** view.
I'll fill the gray areas with your light,
The same way you seem to fill my darkest days.
And I'd draw your face from my perspective,
So that I may never forget
Your eyes,
That chose to see past my fluorescent colored bullcrap
To embrace parts of me that even I couldn't accept
And your lips,
Flushed pink and parted into a smile
That would put even *Mona Lisa* to shame.
But in this game of shades and hues,
I don't understand how an artist
Could ever be satisfied with their work.
I can't comprehend how *Michelangelo*
Was content with the ceiling of the *Sistine Chapel*.

Forget ceilings, I'd go for the stars.
Ask God permission to bless the Heavens
With my **magic marker**
And sketch our story into the constellations
Because our story,
Truly is magic.
But I think I'll remain the tormented artist,
Forever chasing perfection,
Because I paint not knowing if our dreams will one day become a **reality**.
Whether our work will remain nameless in **obscurity**
Or if the images will live on in **immortality**.
But until then, I'll continue to hope and pray
That these watercolors harden into lifelong acrylics.
I'll take our portrait and make copies
Hang the replicas in every art show and museum on the face of this planet
But I'll keep the original and place it in my heart
Because even if one day,
The colors begin to **fade**
And the canvas falls a p a r t,
I'll smile,
Knowing that this masterpiece
Will always be,
Our very own
Work of Art.

I wish I could say that when I met you,
It was *magical.

I wish I could pretend
That the Heavens opened up,
And a light shone down
And a choir of angels
Sang in a perfect three-part harmony.

But they didn't.
There was *no light, no singing,* and definitely, *no angels*.

But believe me,

There was Love…

They told me you were beautiful

You'd twirl strands of thin, brown hair

Around slender fingers,

which, half the time were drawing heart shapes in the sky
Because you knew Love existed way beyond our world.

But for you, Love came in the form of make-believe.

Of summer days pretending to be Dorothy

And being swept away to the magical Land of Oz

Love came from the happiness

Of skipping down that yellow brick road

Without a care in the world

Because fantasy was a lot easier to bear than reality.

And what you had to bear

Was being eight years old

And diagnosed with cancer.

But your answer to that hard blow of reality

Was to keep finding hope

Somewhere over the rainbow.

It was playing hide-and-seek with the little Munchkins

While still going to chemotherapy every other week.

It was focusing on the glimmering lights of the Emerald City

Instead of the blinding glare from your oxygen and I.V.

And it was being able to smile,

Even though Life was like the Wicked Witch of the West

And all she wanted to do
Was keep you **LOCKED** in a hospital bed,

Force-fed through plastic tubes,

And shot drunk with pain killing meds,

Till you were nothing left but dead.

So forgive me when I say that when I met you,

It wasn't *magical.

Because I stood there by your grave for the first time

And I wept for the little girl who had lost her battle to leukemia,

For the Dorothy who never found her way back home to Kansas.

I wept for the big sister that I had never met.

But if only I could go back in time,

I'd tell you not to be afraid

Because even though that "wonderful wizard" couldn't grant you your wishes in the end,

You have more **wit** than any Scarecrow,

More **courage** than any Lion,

And definitely, more **heart** than any Tin Man.

So allow me to continue to draw your heart shapes in the sky

Because now I know that Love truly does exist beyond our world.

And I hope one day, you'll find a pair of ruby red slippers in Heaven Because…

There's no place like home.

There's no place like home..

There's no place like home…

Fanai Castro

is a local writer, poet, artist, and community organizer. She is a co-founder of Sinangån-ta Outreach. Fanai is a regular voice at the Sinangån-ta Poetry Slams and Outreach shows.

Kie Susuico

is a local artist, aspiring poet, and community organizer. He is a member of Inadahen I Lina'la' Kotturan Chamoru Inc. (Guardians of The Chamoru Culture). Kie is a co-founder of Sinangån-ta Poetry Slam & Sinangån-ta Outreach

Melvin Won Pat-Borja

is a local educator, poet, and MC who was a member of the 2003 - 2006 Hawaii Slam Teams. Melvin is the co-founder of Youth Speaks Hawaii. He is also a co-founder of Sinangån-ta Poetry Slam & Sinangån-ta Outreach

Sinangån-ta Outreach

SAINA MA'ASE and THANKS to:

Guam Humanities Council, Sinajana Mayor Roke Blas & Vice Mayor Robert Hofmann, Alex Silverio & The Staff at GUAHAN Project, Dr. Evelyn Flores, Antonio Artero Sablan, Speaker Judi Won Pat & Staff, Dr. Anne Perez Hattori, Anna Palacios, GATE Theater, Pacific Daily News, Marianas Variety, CMAX Construction, Outrigger & Ohana BayView, Hafa Adai Signs, Fokai Industries, N. Santos, Victoria Leon Guerrero, Ronnie Perez, Aaron Tamayo, Jovan Tamayo, Anthony Tamayo for the Photos, John Sabares, and to everybody who helped us out

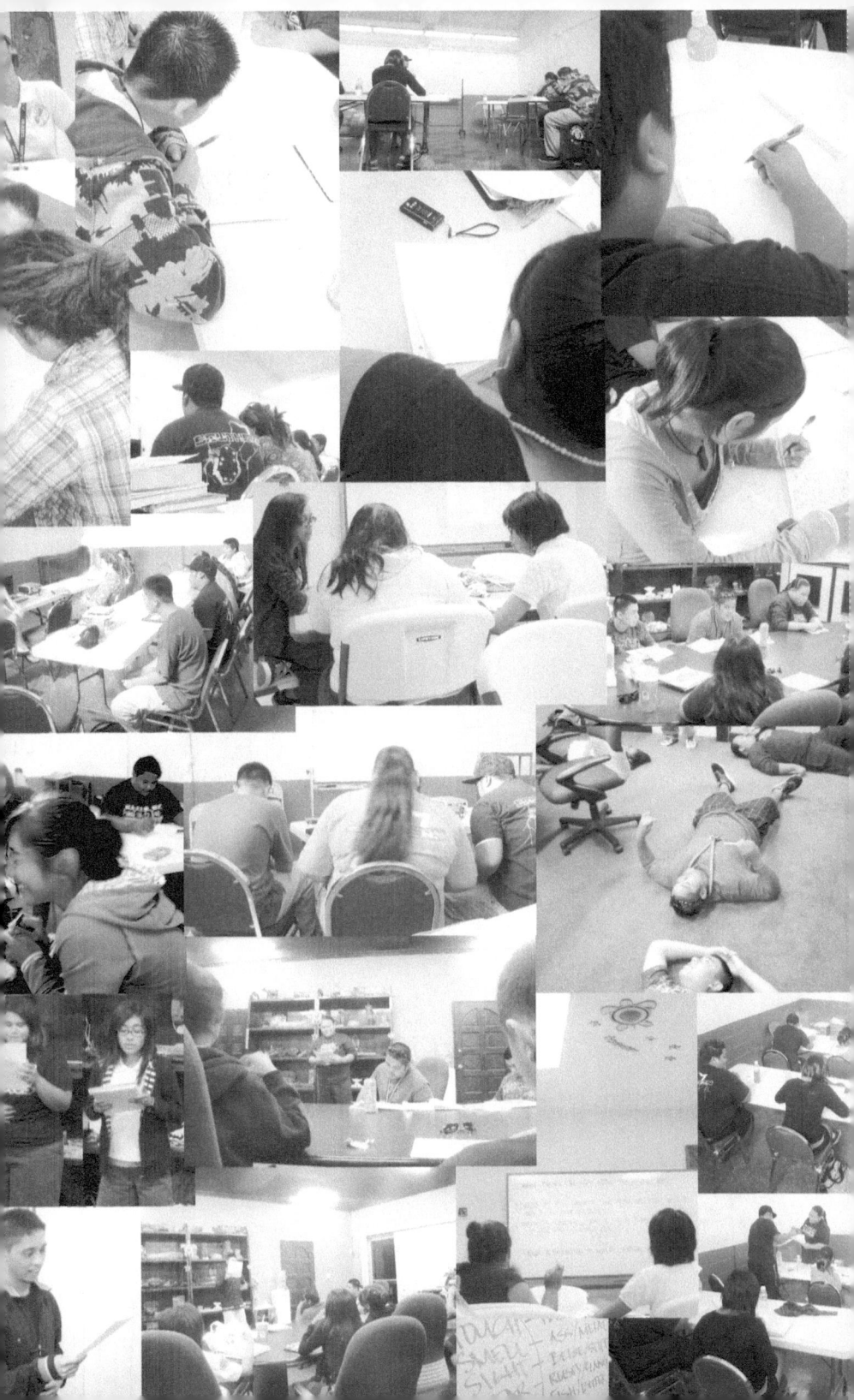

Front Row: John Sarmiento, Vema Zafra, Isha Gabriel, Serena Mañas, Mariah Flores, Ittai Wong, Shang Salas, Jessie Rae Tedtaotao, Aaron Tamayo, Melvin Wong, Pat-Borja. **Back Row:** Alaka'i Kotrys, Peter Santos, William Giles, Chanice Guevara, Asa Gonzalez, Kie Susuico, Ronnie Perez. **Not Pictured:** Christian Camacho, Chelsea Santos, Fanai Castro.

www.ingramcontent.com/pod-product-compliance
Lightning Source LLC
Chambersburg PA
CBHW020325130626
46549CB00003B/1019